Davy Crockett

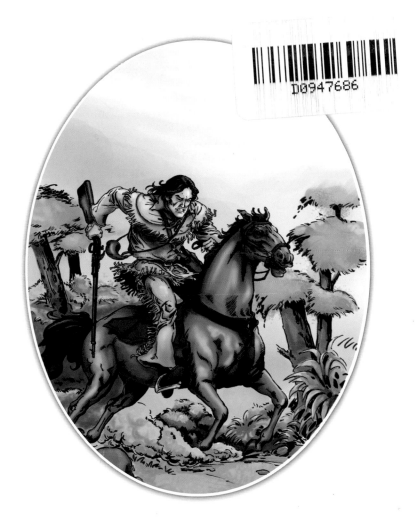

SADDLEBACK
EDUCATIONAL PUBLISHING

Saddleback's Graphic Biographies

SADDLEBACK
EDUCATIONAL PUBLISHING
www.sdlback.com

ISBN-13: 978-1-59905-220-5
ISBN-10: 1-59905-220-2
eBook: 978-1-60291-583-1

Printed in Guangzhou, China
1011/CA21101634

15 14 13 12 11   3 4 5 6 7 8 9

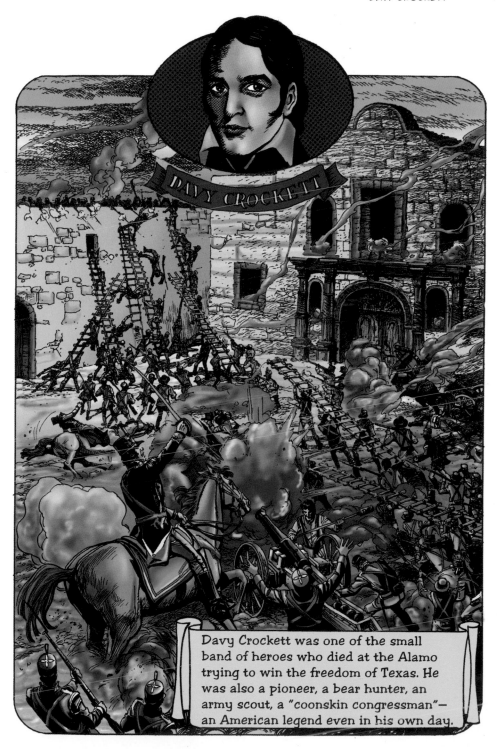

Davy Crockett was one of the small band of heroes who died at the Alamo trying to win the freedom of Texas. He was also a pioneer, a bear hunter, an army scout, a "coonskin congressman"— an American legend even in his own day.

It was 1786, a few years after Daniel Boone led settlers into Kentucky. A band of Native Americans attacked a cabin on another part of the frontier, which would soon become Tennessee.

The owner, David Crockett, and his family were killed.

A short time later, only a few miles away, a ninth child was born to his son, John Crockett.

A boy! I want to name him David in memory of my father.

And we'll call him Davy!

Davy learned early how to handle a rifle.

You're eight years old, son. Think you can hunt game by yourself?

Yes, sir!

Take my rifle and go hunting whenever you want. But you're to take only one bullet with you.

Any time you miss your shot, you'll go to bed with no supper!

Y-yes, sir.

Davy soon became an expert in a country full of sharpshooters. He grew up. He liked dances. He met a girl named Polly Finley.

There's a shooting match coming up, Polly. If I could win the prize, I'd have a question to ask you.

I'll be waiting, Davy, and cheering for you.

More than eighty men entered the contest. The first prize was a live steer.

Each man has one shot at 50 yards distance. The top shooter will try again at 75 yards.

4

Davy used a rifle called "old Betsey." He reached the final test at 100 yards.

I can hit that bull's-eye with one eye closed. Come on, old Betsey.

A bull's-eye, the winner is young Crockett!

Davy sold his prize steer for five gold dollars. He went to Polly's house.

I'd like mighty well to change your name from Polly Finley to Mrs. David Crockett.

And I'd like that too!

Two weeks later they were married. They moved to their new home.

It's lovely Davy, our own home!

Just as long as I pay the twenty-five cents a month rent!

A year was long enough. There was a new baby boy. And Davy was restless.

I want my children to grow up in a new country. There's fine land for the taking in south Tennessee. Wild, great hunting.

How far away? How would we get there?

A week's travel by boat would do it. We'll take the spinning wheel and loom, the horses and dogs, you and the baby.

By the next spring, Polly agreed. And there were two babies. They went to the nearest riverboat dock.

Hey Captain, you got room for us?

Sure have! Come right aboard!

The big ark floated down the Holston and into the big Tennessee River. They slept in bunks in the cabin. Other passengers came and left again.

Look at that deer! This is a great gaming country.

They reached the end of the boat trip and went on shore.

Where do we go now?

There's a trail over the mountains and down into the Elk River Valley.

It was fine weather. They camped along the trail.

Here's dinner! Is the pot ready? Never did I see so much game!

In a few days, they were home. Davy built a small cabin.

It's a good cabin.

Only a dirt floor, but I'll soon cover it with bear skin rugs.

In the next year Davy killed 105 bears.

All right, easy, steady ...

Soon people all over knew that Davy was a great hunter.

Word spread all over Tennessee.

That young Davy Crockett's killed enough bear to feed every scout in the country!

And enough raccoons to make caps for every man and boy!

But the year was 1813, there was other news.

We're at war with England again. And the English are stirring up the Creek to kill settlers.

At Fort Mims in Alabama, Creek warriors wiped out a whole settlement of men, women, and children. That's wrong! Maybe the country can use another sharpshooter.

Oh Davy! Don't go to war!

My granddad fought the redcoats, my father too. I guess it's my turn to go. It won't be for long, Polly.

So Davy went off with his gun, leaving his dogs behind for once. He headed to the camp where other volunteers were gathering.

It's a good place for a camp, but where's the army?

They're on the way. General Andrew Jackson's bringing them.

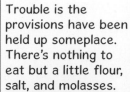

Trouble is the provisions have been held up someplace. There's nothing to eat but a little flour, salt, and molasses.

No meat? I can get you some. There are signs of bear around here.

I've heard you were the best bear hunter in Tennessee.

Colonel, that's a lie! I'm the best bear hunter on earth!

Davy took a few men and left camp. Soon General Jackson arrived with an army.

I've brought plenty of guns and powder but not much food.

I'm sorry, General Jackson. We've received no provisions here!

Jackson's famous temper was about to explode, when suddenly there was a lot of noise and a strange parade.

It's Davy Crockett, the Tennessee bear hunter.

And a good 500 pounds of bear! The men won't go to bed hungry.

Soon the General had 1,500 men. His job was to fight the Native Americans. But he was worried.

Every day there are more reports of attacks, but my men don't know how to drill. They've never been under fire. They need training!

We can wait no longer. How many good fighting men could you pick out of this bunch?

Would fifty help?

Coffee was put in charge of the fifty men with Major Russell and Scout Crockett under him. They were to find the warriors.

For a month they tracked warrior raiding parties with no luck. Then ...

He says there is a camp of Creeks about a day's ride away. He'll guide us part way.

Saddle your horses!

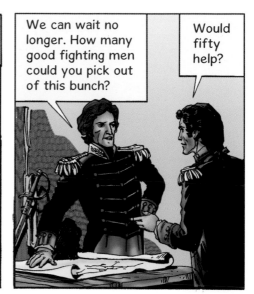

At dawn the next day, Coffee and his men attacked. Bullets and arrows whistled through the air.

In ten minutes the battle was over. Thirty-eight Creek warriors were dead. The rest disappeared into the woods, leaving only women and children behind.

Davy was the only one who knew the Creek language.

The women think they will be killed.

Nonsense! Tell them to bring their things. We'll take them to the army camp.

Back at the main camp there was a new problem.

This man says 200 friendly Native Americans and several white families are at Fort Talladega, surrounded by 1,100 Creek warriors.

The Creeks said that unless those in the Fort joined them against the settlers, they would kill them all. Jackson started his army on the move.

He sent his scouts ahead quickly to look things over.

The Creeks can take that fort anytime they try!

They're telling the Native Americans in the fort how bad it'll be if they don't come out by tomorrow!

We've got to help them. They're on our side! I'll ride back and find General Jackson!

By moonlight Davy rode fast through the woods.

I'm a good target if the Creeks have scouts posted.

He found Jackson's camp six miles back. Quickly the General told 500 mounted men to follow Crockett. They reached the fort after sunrise.

Bravely, Russell and his men advanced. The Creeks laid an ambush in thick bushes. They rushed out to attack.

Then Crockett and his men attacked from behind. When the Creeks ran, they met Hammond's rifles coming from the other side.

The army moved to a new camp. Jackson sent the scouts to find out what the warriors were up to. They reported back to him.

A strong enemy force is gathered on the Tallapoosa River, close to a horseshoe bend.

They expect us to cross there. There's a narrow gorge* near the bend. I'll bet it's filled with a thousand of them waiting to ambush us.

We'll cross five miles downstream. It's harder, but we'll surprise them and attack from the other side.

At first things went as planned. The main army crossed the river. The artillery crossed, then the scouts.

Major, the warriors! They're attacking from behind us!

They had learned of Jackson's plans. They made a surprise attack from the rear, catching the scouts in midstream, under a hail of arrows and bullets.

* gorge, a narrow passage or canyon

The American troops on the other bank had not been in battle before. Instead of firing, they ran for the woods.

Come back, you cowards!

Charging through the water, the scouts forced their way ashore and into hand-to-hand combat with the warriors.

Colonel Carroll brought up men to replace the green troops.

Steady, men! Aim the cannon.

General Jackson himself came back to help fire the cannon.

Give it to them hot and heavy!

The cannon fire on top of the scouts' charge was too much for the Native American warriors. They broke ranks and ran.

The Tallapoosa River battle was nearly the end of the war with the Creeks. Soon they signed a peace treaty.

Davy did not like the treaty.

I've killed many a Creek warrior, but now I'm sorry. This treaty we've forced on them is not fair.

I'm an army man, Davy. I do what I'm told.

I'm a hunter and a fighter, but I guess I'm no army man. I'll be glad to get out of it.

From then on, Davy was a friend of the Native Americans.

He received an honorable discharge from the army and went home. The children were well, but not his Polly.

I'll be well in no time, now that you're home, Davy!

Instead, Polly soon died. Sadly, Davy buried her and marked her grave with a big limestone boulder.

Elizabeth Patton, a war widow with two children, lived nearby. Her cabin was lonely without a husband. Davy's cabin was lonely without Polly.

After a while, Davy proposed to Elizabeth.

Why don't we get married and make one big happy family?

That suits me fine, Davy!

The Crockett family moved farther west. Their new neighbors were forming a militia company.

We'd be proud to have such a famous scout for our militia, Colonel.

Then they elected Colonel Crockett a judge.

A judge needs to read law and write judgments. I'll have to work on it.

Davy dammed up his creek and built the first mill in the neighborhood.

Mighty handy to get my corn and wheat ground so close to home!

With the hunting so poor, man has to do something.

He was elected to the state legislature. When he came home, a flood had washed his mill away.

Don't worry, dear. We'll sell everything, pay our debts, and move west.

That's the kind of talk I like. Maybe we can find a place where the hunting's still good!

In 1822 they settled in Gibson County near the Tennessee River.

Greatest country I ever saw! There's bear, deer, cougar, mink, beaver, otters, and raccoons! And the nearest neighbor's eight miles away!

Will you teach us to hunt, Pa?

I'll teach you all I know about it!

For the next few years, Davy often took his sons with him into the woods.

The Tennessee bear hunter was becoming known all over the country. Strangers often stopped to hear his stories.

I've heard that you hunt alligators too, Mr. Crockett.

Well, yes, I like to tame alligators and make pets of them. I'd rather ride on a gator than in a canoe. Faster ride, less work.

Two of the strangers had a different question.

Crockett, you're a well-known man. Why not run for Congress?

Right now I've got some bear hunting to do, and I've started a barrel-stave business. Come around later and I might say yes.

Water pipes and barrels were made of wooden staves wired together. Davy had a crew of men cutting trees and making staves. Another crew was building flat boats.

I figure on floating 30,000 staves down the Mississippi to New Orleans on the two boats.

Davy and his men were landlubbers. He hired Captain Whale to pilot the boats.

Welcome, Captain! I understand you're one of the best pilots on the Mississippi.

That's true, Mr. Crockett, if I do say so myself.

But on the big, tricky Mississippi, Captain Whale did not seem to know what to do.

Well, I ... I was an assistant pilot once!

Were you ever a pilot on this river?

Davy had both boats lashed together. Night came.

When are we going to tie up for the night?

Well, uh, pretty soon.

But Whale did not know how to bring the boat to shore! And on a bad part of the river known as the Devil's Elbow, they crashed into an island.

Every man for himself!

Every one reached the island safely, though shaken and bruised. Davy made a speech.

Boys, the people of west Tennessee demand I save them and save the country by running for Congress!

I plan to have a law passed keeping fools from going into the wood stave business; and another law for the hanging of fake river pilots.

Home again, Davy went hunting. Then he took a bundle of furs to the store to trade.

There's mink, otter, wildcat ... How come no coonskins?

I'm saving the coonskins. I plan to run for Congress this fall.

I figure I'll need a couple of fine new coonskin caps when I get to Washington!

Sounds like you're sure you're going to win!

Davy did win. He had a lot of friends, and they got out the vote for him. He came in first by a good majority.

In his first term in Congress, Davy kept quiet and learned. But in Washington and in the newspapers, he got a lot of attention.

Who in the world is that?

That's Davy Crockett, the coonskin Congressman from Tennessee.

How would you describe yourself, Congressman?

Why I'm David Crockett, fresh from the backwoods—half horse, half alligator, a little touched with snapping turtle.

I can wade the Mississippi, leap the Ohio, ride a streak of lightening, whip my weight in wildcats, hug a bear too close for comfort, and beat any man opposed to Jackson.

Davy was proud of General Andrew Jackson when he became President. In Davy's second term, when certain bills came up, he took the opposite side from Jackson.

Gold had been discovered on Native American lands in several southern states. These states now demanded that the lands be taken away from the Native Americans.

Those lands belonged to the Native Americans before the white man ever came here! They were guaranteed by the treaty at the end of the Creek war. It is wrong to take them away.

But a bill was introduced in Congress that would move the Native Americans to new lands west of the Mississippi.

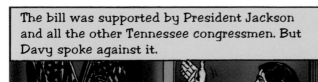

The bill was supported by President Jackson and all the other Tennessee congressmen. But Davy spoke against it.

It is not justice! I would rather be an old coon dog belonging to a poor man in the forest than belong to any party that will not do justice to all!

The people at home did not care about the Native Americans. Davy was not re-elected. But in 1833 he was sent back to Congress.

This time he was a champion of the new Whig party. They sent him on a tour of cities. In Philadelphia they gave him a new, silver-trimmed rifle.

Colonel Crockett, the Whig gentlemen of Philadelphia salute you.

In New York ...

Colonel Crockett, our great city is yours! Here is the key!

And in Boston ...

Colonel Crockett, our great city is honored.

But the people at home did not like it.

You voting for Colonel Crocket again?

Not me! Like the newspapers say, he's turned Yankee.

In a close election, Davy Crockett was defeated.

He was angry. He felt the Tennessee people had let him down.

If they don't want me in Tennessee, I'll go explore Texas. Something big is going on down there!

They've rebelled against Mexico. They're fighting for their freedom. They want volunteers.

I wish I could go along, Pa.

Davy left in November 1835. He traveled through Arkansas. He reached Nacogdoches, Texas, in January 1836.

Welcome, Colonel Crockett, to the Republic of Texas.

Greetings to you from the state of Tennessee!

Later, after a celebration in his honor, Davy heard the latest news.

On January 14, Crockett signed an oath before Judge John Forbes to the Provisional Government of Texas.

Volunteers are gathering at San Antonio. We've held the town since December.

If you want volunteers for your army, why not sign me up?

We're proud to have you! We'll make you a Texas Colonel! Sign here.

No, no! Just make me a kind of high private!

Davy rode southwest to San Antonio. He reached the Alamo, an old Spanish mission used as a fort, at night.

Who are you, stranger?

Davy Crockett of Tennessee, half-horse and half-alligator!

Jim Bowie rushed out to welcome Davy and took him inside.

He's here! Turn out, everybody, to meet Davy Crockett of Tennessee.

Colonel Travis and Colonel Bowie told him how things stood.

Santa Anna, the Mexican commander, is almost to Texas with his troops

He has cannons too. We only have 150 men at the Alamo.

But this is our first line of defense! Every day we can hold Santa Anna's army here is a day longer for the main Texas army to arm and get ready.

Then we better hold the Alamo.

The Mexican army arrived and took up positions around the Alamo. Santa Anna sent a demand: *Surrender or die!*

Travis replied: "No surrender!" The siege of the Alamo began.

Make every shot count, men.

As the days passed there was no sleep. The defenders ran to one wall, and then another as the Mexicans raised ladders.

Quick, to the west wall!

Ammunition ran low.

Two more rounds, then I start using nails!

It's as bad as that?

At the end, it was hand-to-hand combat. The defenders fought with guns, knives, and fists until not a man among them remained alive.

They had stopped Santa Anna's army for twelve days. Thousands of brave Mexican soldiers died. Santa Anna had other men, but those he lost at the Alamo were his best troops.

Seven weeks later at San Jacinto, General Sam Houston and the Texas army wiped out the Mexican army. They charged with a new battle cry.

Remember the Alamo!

Part of the Alamo still stands in San Antonio today. Davy Crockett was one of the small band of heroes who died there to win independence for Texas.

Pioneer, bear hunter, army scout, and coonskin Congressman, Davy Crockett was an American legend even in his own day.

The End

Saddleback's Graphic Fiction & Nonfiction

If you enjoyed this Graphic Biography ... you will also enjoy our other graphic titles including:

Graphic Classics

- Around the World in Eighty Days
- The Best of Poe
- Black Beauty
- The Call of the Wild
- A Christmas Carol
- A Connecticut Yankee in King Arthur's Court
- Dr. Jekyll and Mr. Hyde
- Dracula
- Frankenstein
- The Great Adventures of Sherlock Holmes
- Gulliver's Travels
- Huckleberry Finn
- The Hunchback of Notre Dame
- The Invisible Man
- Jane Eyre
- Journey to the Center of the Earth
- Kidnapped
- The Last of the Mohicans
- The Man in the Iron Mask
- Moby Dick
- The Mutiny On Board H.M.S. Bounty
- The Mysterious Island
- The Prince and the Pauper
- The Red Badge of Courage
- The Scarlet Letter
- The Swiss Family Robinson
- A Tale of Two Cities
- The Three Musketeers
- The Time Machine
- Tom Sawyer
- Treasure Island
- 20,000 Leagues Under the Sea
- The War of the Worlds

Graphic Shakespeare

- As You Like It
- Hamlet
- Julius Caesar
- King Lear
- Macbeth
- The Merchant of Venice
- A Midsummer Night's Dream
- Othello
- Romeo and Juliet
- The Taming of the Shrew
- The Tempest
- Twelfth Night

SADDLEBACK
EDUCATIONAL PUBLISHING